SPOT THE DIFFERENCES
NATICALITIES

by FUNNYLANGUAGES

Australia

Capital City: Canberra
Official language: English

Interesting facts

1. Australia is both a country and a continent;

2. Canberra, the capital city of Australia, was built between Sydney and Melbourne, as they could not decide which city should be the capital;

3. In Australian English there are some unique words, for example: *Aussie* means Australian, *barbie* means barbeque, *brekky* means breakfast, *chook* means chicken;

4. Kangaroos can be found only in Australia. The population of kangaroos in the country outnumbers the human population;

5. Australian Dingo Fence or Dog Fence is the longest fence in the world. It is nearly 2 meters high and stretches 5,530 kilometers across Australia.

Spot 15 differences

In the upper picture:

There are two (1)**b** _ _ _ _ _ behind the surfer. There is a (2)**b** _ _ _ in the kangaroo's pocket. There is (3)**h** _ _ _ under the bandana. There is a (4)**w** _ _ _ in the sea. There is a white (5)**s** _ _ _ on the kangaroo's tail. The surfer's (6) **n** _ _ _ is bigger. There is a white spot on the kangaroo's (7)**h** _ _ _.

In the bottom picture:

The (8)**s** _ _ is on the right. There is an (9)**e**_ _ _ _ _ _ _ _ _ _ tree. The colour of the (10)**b** _ _ _ _ _ _ on the surfer's head. The colour of the (11)**b** _ _ _ _ _ the surfer holds. The length of the kanagaroo's (12)**t** _ _ _. The (13)**c** _ _ _ _ _ and the (14)**l** _ _ _ _ _ of swimming trunks. The colour of the (15)**e** _ _ _ is different.

Brazil

Capital City: Brasilia
Official language: Portuguese

Interesting facts

1. Brazil's capital Brasilia looks like an aeroplane from above;

2. The island of Ilha da Queimada Grande or Snake island, which belongs to Brazil, is the deadliest place on earth. It is full of venomous snakes;

3. Brazil is home to the largest population of Japanese people outside Japan;

4. Rio de Janeiro hosts the world's largest carnival, annually held in the first week of March;

5. Brazilian prisoners are allowed to reduce their sentence by four days for every book that they read.

Spot 17 differences

In the upper picture:

The feathers of the dress are of different (1)c _ _ _ _ _ _ _. The woman is wearing (2)e _ _ _ _ _ _ _ _. The top on the woman is (3)p _ _ _. The woman is wearing different (4)s _ _ _ _ _. The (5) b _ _ _ _ _ _ _ are of different colours. The design and the (6) c _ _ _ _ _ of the man's hat is different. The man is wearing a (7)s _ _ _ _ of different design and colour. There is a (8)b _ _ _ on the man's waist. There is a maraca in the (9)h _ _ _ of the man.

In the bottom picture:

The woman has a different (10)h _ _ . The top on the woman has a different (11)d _ _ _ _ _ _. The woman is wearing a burgundy (12) s _ _ _ _. The quantity of (13)b _ _ _ _ _ _ _ . The man is holding the (14)b _ _ _ _ _ _ in the other hand. The man is wearing a light (15) b _ _ _ jumpsuit. The man is wearing (16)s _ _ _ _. There are two (17)d _ _ _ in the picture.

Canada

Capital City: Ottawa
Official languages: English, French

Interesting facts

1. Canada is the largest country in the Western hemisphere in terms of area and the second largest country in the world after Russia;

2. Canada has two official languages: English and French. Montreal is the world's second largest French-speaking city after Paris;

3. Canadian one-dollar coin is called the "loonie" and the two-dollar coin is called the "toonie";

4. 60% of the world's polar bear population is in Canada;

5. The baseball glove was invented in Canada in 1883.

Spot 15 differences

In the upper picture:

There is a different (1)s _ _ _ _ of the gate. There is a (2)g _ _ _ _ pompom on the beaver's hat. The beaver has shields of different (3)c _ _ _ _ _. The (4) p _ _ _ is near the player, not in the net. The colour of the beaver's (5)s _ _ _ _ is different. There is a blue (6) s _ _ _ _ _ on the player sweater. The maple (7)l _ _ _ is yellow. The beaver has two (8)t _ _ _ _not one.

In the bottom picture:

The corners of the gate cross-bars are (9)r _ _ . The colour of beaver's (10)t _ _ _ is different. There is a brown spot on the beaver's (11)p _ _ . The stick's lacing has different (12)c _ _ _ _ _ _. There is a (13)m _ _ _ _ on the player's chest. The (14)h _ _ _ _ _ on the player's head is grey. The beaver has brown (15)s _ _ _ _ _ _.

China

Capital City: Beijing
Official language: Chinese

Interesting facts

1. Chinese New Year is the biggest holiday in China. Chinese New Year's celebration lasts for 15 days!

2. Spitting, yawning, grunting, and burping are not considered rude in China;

3. Every single panda that lives in this world belongs to China;

4. The bristle toothbrush was invented in 1498 by a Chinese who made toothbrushes with coarse horse hairs attached to bone or bamboo handles;

5. The umbrella was invented in China 3500 years ago.

Spot 16 differences

In the upper picture:

The woman's (1)**d** _ _ _ _ is red. The man's plait is located on the other (2)**s** _ _ _ _ _ _ _. There are two (3)**d** _ _ _ _ _ _ on the umbrella. The woman is holding the (4)**u** _ _ _ _ _ _ _ in the other hand. The man's hat is (5)**g** _ _ _ _. The man has a sparse (6)**b** _ _ _ _. The man's (7)**p** _ _ _ _ are red. There are blue and green stripes on the edge of the (8)**u** _ _ _ _ _ _ _.

In the bottom picture:

The (9)**r** _ _ _ of the man is red. The man's plait is (10)**t** _ _ _ _ _ _ and shorter. The pagoda has one less (11)**t** _ _ _. The (12)**p** _ _ _ _ _ _ of the dress is different. There are two separate (13)**w** _ _ _ _ _ _ on the ground floor of the pagoda. The man has white cuffs on his (14) **s** _ _ _ _ _ _. The button facing on the robe is (15)**b** _ _ _. There is no (16)**t** _ _ tree near the man.

Denmark

Capital City: Copenhagen
Official language: Danish

Interesting facts

1. One could reach the ocean by travelling just 52 km from any point in the country;

2. Denmark is a flat country. The tallest hill is a mere 170 meters high;

3. There are more bicycles than people in Copenhagen. The citizens of Copenhagen daily pedal a combined 1 million km;

4. Bluetooth got its name from Denmark's second King – Harald Bluetooth;

5. Denmark is the home of Lego. The name "lego" is a shortening of the Danish term "leg godt", which translates as 'play well'.

Spot 16 differences

In the upper picture:

The woman's (1)**j** _ _ _ _ _ is black. The (2)**a** _ _ _ _ has two laces. The woman is holding (3)**f** _ _ _ _ _ _ _. Woman's shoes are (4)**r** _ _ not blue. The boy has green (5)**s** _ _ _ _. The boy is holding a (6) **b** _ _ _ Lego brick. The boy is holding a (7)**c** _ _ _ _ _ _ in the other hand. The woman's (8)**h** _ _ _ is tied up in a bun.

In the bottom picture:

The woman is wearing a (9)**s** _ _ _ _ _. The jacket of the woman has short (10)**s** _ _ _ _ _ _ _. There is a (11)**b** _ _ _ _ _ in the woman's hand. The woman's (12)**h** _ _ _ is raised. The boy is wearing long (13)**p** _ _ _ _. The boy's right hand is on his (14)**w** _ _ _ _ _. The woman is wearing a (15)**h** _ _. There are two rows of (16)**b** _ _ _ _ _ _ on the boy's vest.

England

Capital City: London
Official language: English

Interesting facts

1. England is the largest part of the Great Britan;

2. 1 billion people speak English. That's 1 in every 7 on the Earth;

3. French was the official language of England for about 300 years, from 1066 till 1362;

4. There is a funny competition in England: people roll wheels of cheese down a hill, and see whose cheese gets to the bottom first;

5. Another weird competition is a lying competition. Competitors have five minutes to tell the biggest and most convincing lie.

Spot 16 differences

In the upper picture:

The guard post is (1)**b** _ _ _ not green. There are two (2)**s** _ _ _ _ _ _ on the post rim. The man is holding a (3)**b** _ _ _ _ _ _ not dachshund. The man is holding a brown (4)**u** _ _ _ _ _ _ _, not a red one. There are (5)**c** _ _ _ _ _ on the jacket. There is a (6)**p** _ _ _ _ _ on the jacket. There is the (7)**s** _ _ and one (8)**c** _ _ _ _ in the sky.

In the bottom picture:

The roof of the post is (9)**y** _ _ _ _ _. There are yellow (10) **s** _ _ _ _ _ _ on the post roof. The guard is (11)**i** _ _ _ _ _ the post. There are storm (12)**c** _ _ _ _ _ _ . The (13)**u** _ _ _ _ _ _ _ _ is opened. The jacket is (14)**b** _ _ _ not green. The pants are green not (15)**b** _ _ _ _. The (16)**p** _ _ _ _ are not creased.

Finland

Capital City: Helsinki
Official language: Finnish

Interesting facts

1. Finland was a part of Sweden for almost 600 years and a part of Russia for about 100 years;

2. The Finnish language is unrelated to Scandinavian languages. It is part of the Uralic language family, of which Hungarian is the closest;

3. There are approximately 2.2 million saunas in Finland. That's one sauna for every two and a half people;

4. You can still find people in Finland who were born in the sauna. Previously, it was believed that the sauna was the only sterile place;

5. The Finns don't have a dishwashing sponge. They have a dishwashing brush instead.

Spot 16 differences

In the upper picture:

The deer's antlers are (1)**g** _ _ _. There is a pattern on the (2)**h** _ _. There is no (3)**s** _ _ _ on the top of the fir tree. The (4)**s** _ _ _ _ is coming out of the chimney. There are two (5)**w** _ _ _ _ _ _ _ on the facade of the building on the second floor. There is a (6)**b** _ _ _ _ _ _ on the snowman. The (7)**s** _ _ _ _ _ _ _ looks towards the barrel. There are two (8)**b** _ _ _ _ _ _ _ on the snowman.

On the bottom picture:

The antlers have a different (9)**s** _ _ _ _ _. The (10)**b** _ _ _ _ _ _ is smaller. There is a fir tree on the (11)**h** _ _ _. There are two (12)**f** _ _ _ _ _ _ _ near the house. There is a (13)**s** _ _ _ _ _ in front of the house. There is a (14)**h** _ _ on the snowman. The snowman has (15)**t** _ _ _ _ as hands. The deer has a grey (16) **n** _ _ _.

France

Capital City: Paris
Official language: French

Interesting facts

1. French is the official language of 29 countries in the world;

2. French fries is not a French invention. It's the Belgians who invented fries;

3. The French believe that placing a baguette (or any type of bread) upside down on a table can cause bad luck;

4. The French consider snails to be a delicacy. They eat about 25,000 tons of snails a year;

5. Over half of all roundabouts in the world are in France.

Spot 16 differences

In the upper picture:

Eiffel Tower is in the (1)**m** _ _ _ _ _ of the picture. The woman is wearing a red top and an (2)**o** _ _ _ _ _ _ skirt . The woman is wearing blue (3)**s** _ _ _ _. The woman has different (4)**h** _ _ _ _ _ _. There is no baguette in the (5)**b** _ _ _ _ _. The bike is (6)**p** _ _ _ _ _ _. There is a (7)**w** _ _ _ _ on the woman's wrist. There is French (8)**f** _ _ _ on the Eiffel Tower.

In the bottom picture:

The man and the woman swapped (9)**p** _ _ _ _ _ _. The woman is wearing a pink (10)**d** _ _ _ _. The man is wearing an (11)**o** _ _ _ _ _ _ beret. The man is eating a (12)**c** _ _ _ _ _ _ _ _ _. The man's pant (13) **l** _ _ is rolled up. Man's (14)**s** _ _ _ _ is tied differently. There is a (15)**b** _ _ _ _ _ in the basket. The bike's handles are (16)**g** _ _ _ _.

Germany

Capital City: Berlin
Official language: German

Interesting facts

1. Berlin is 9 times bigger than Paris and has more bridges than Venice;

2. There are 35 dialects in German language;

3. If someone asks you if you would like a drink, you should say "bitte" (please), if you want it and "danke" (thanks) if you don't;

4. Germany has 1,000 varieties of sausages;

5. The first printed book was in German.

Spot 14 differences

In the upper picture:

There are two (1)h_ _ _ _ _ _ in the picture. There are no (2)f_ _ _ _ _ _ under the attic window. The (3)d_ _ _ is red not green. The woman is wearing a (4)h_ _. The pants are (5)b_ _ _ _ _. The (6)p_ _ _ _ are short. There are no folds on the (7)a_ _ _ _ _.

In the bottom picture:

There are two separate (8)w_ _ _ _ _ _ _ on the ground floor. There is a (9)t_ _ _ _ in front of the house. There is a (10)t_ _ _ behind the Germans. The (11)f_ _ _ _ _ _ _ is on the other side of the hat. There are two (12)b_ _ _ _ _ _ _ on the pants. The woman is holding a (13)g_ _ _ _ of beer. There are two bundles of (14)s_ _ _ _ _ _ _ _.

India

Capital City: New Delhi
Official languages: Hindi, English

Interesting facts

1. India has 22 official languages;

2. Hinglish is a mix of Hindi (the official language of India) and English;

3. Cows are holy in India. That's why you hardly can find beef there;

4. Police officers are given higher pay for having a mustache;

5. Indian farmers use Coca-Cola and Pepsi as pesticides.

Spot 17 differences

In the upper picture:

The snake charmer folded his (1)**l**_ _ _ differently. The (2)**s**_ _ _ _ _ has blue buttons. There are buttons on the (3)**s**_ _ _ _ _. The old man has a long (4)**b**_ _ _ _. The (5)**e**_ _ _ _ _ _ _ _ is looking in the different direction. There is a (6)**p**_ _under the snake charmer. There is no (7)**T-s**_ _ _ _ under the charmer's shirt. There are six wrinkles on the elephant (8)**t**_ _ _ _. The charmer's hat is (9)**b**_ _ _.

In the bottom picture:

The shirt of the snake charmer is (10)**o**_ _ _ _ _ _. There are only two (11)**b**_ _ _ _ _ _ _ on the shirt. The (12)**T-s**_ _ _ _ _ of the old man is light blue. The elephant's (13)**t**_ _ _ is located differently. The elephant's (14)**f**_ _ _ _ _ _ is thicker. The snake is (15)**c**_ _ _ _ _ to the charmer. The shirt is covering man's (16)**l**_ _ _. The charmer has a (17)**m**_ _ _ _ _ _ _ _.

Italy

Capital City: Rome
Official language: Italian

Interesting facts

1. Italy is shaped like a high boot;

2. Pasta was first brought to Italy in the 13th century by Arab merchants. It was served with honey and sugar and eaten with fingers!

3. A popular Italian dessert Tiramisú can be translated into English as "pick me up";

4. One of the narrowest streets in the world can be found in Venice. It measures just 53 cm wide!

5. In Italy, the number 13 is actually considered good luck. It's the number 17 that Italians consider bad luck.

Spot 15 differences

In the upper picture:

The (1)**T**_ _ _ _ of Pisa is on the right. The (2)**c**_ _ is red not yellow. There is a (3)**p**_ _ _ _ in the man's hand. The pants are (4)**g**_ _ _ _ not blue. The scarf coloured as Italian (5)**f**_ _ _. The (6)**m**_ _ has a fringe. The colour of the (7)**s**_ _ _ _ is different. There is a (8)**l**_ _ _ on the car door.

In the bottom picture:

The (9)**c**_ _ is on the right. The (10)**h**_ _ _ _ _ _ _ _ _ _ of the car are smaller. The man's (11)**p**_ _ _ _ are shorter. The man's (12)**s**_ _ _ _ is red not blue. Light blue dots on the rim of the (13)**p**_ _ _ _ _. The man's (14)**h**_ _ _ is shorter. The shape of (15)**e**_ _ _ _ _ _ _ is different.

Japan

Capital City: Tokyo
Official language: Japanese

Interesting facts

1. Japan consists of over 6,800 islands, but only 430 of these are inhabited;

2. The highest mountain in Japan is Mount Fuji, a dormant (sleeping) volcano;

3. Japanese people often find it difficult to apologize. So, in Japan you can pay a specialized agency who can do it for you;

4. Black cats are believed to bring good luck in Japan;

5. Japanese have a tradition of visiting KFC on Christmas Eve.

Spot 16 differences

In the upper picture:

The (1)k_ _ _ _ _ of the woman is pink. The (2)p_ _ _ _ _ _ _ of the fan is different. The woman has different (3)h_ _ _ _ _ _. The belt is (4)p_ _ _. The shape of the (5)t_ _ _ is different. The (6)s_ _ _ _ garden is on the right side of the picture. The man is in the (7)m_ _ _ _ _ of the picture. The woman's (8)s_ _ _ _ are pink.

In the bottom picture:

The pattern of the (9)k_ _ _ _ _ _ is different. There is a (10)h_ _ _ _ _ _ _ in the woman's hair. The (11)b_ _ _ of the kimono is different. There are two (12)t_ _ _ _ behind the woman. There are more (13)s_ _ _ _ _ in the stone garden. The (14)s_ _ _ _ is coming from Fudji. There are stripes on the man's (15)p_ _ _ _. The scabbard is (16)b_ _ _ _ _.

Mexico

Capital City: Mexico City
Official language: Spanish

Interesting facts

1. 69 different languages are spoken in Mexico;

2. Ancient Mexico can be said to have produced five major civilizations: the Olmec, Maya, Teotihuacan, Toltec and Aztec;

3. The world's smallest dog is named after Mexican state Chihuahua;

4. Chocolate, chilies and corn were introduced to the world by Mexico;

5. In 1913, Mexico had three different presidents, in a span of one hour.

Spot 16 differences

In the upper picture:

The sombrero is (1)b_ _ _ _. The (2)d_ _ _ _ _ of the sombrero is different. The (3)s_ _ _ _ is multicoloured. The man is wearing a (4)y_ _ _ _ _ band. The (5)h_ _ _ of the man is turned into a different direction. There are less appendages on the left (6) c_ _ _ _ _. There are two (7)f_ _ _ _ _ _ on the right cactus. The sun is on the (8)r_ _ _ _ part of the picture.

In the bottom picture:

The (9)s_ _ _ _ _ _ _ has a different pattern. The man is wearing a (10)j_ _ _ _ _. The pants are (11)g_ _ _. The lampas have a different (12)c_ _ _ _ _. The man is holding a (13)t_ _ _ instead of maraca. There are no small (14)c_ _ _ _ _ with a (15)f_ _ _ _ _ on the left. The man has long and thin (16)m_ _ _ _ _ _ _ _.

Mongolia

Capital City: Ulaanbaatar
Official language: Mongolian

Interesting facts

1. In 13th century the Mongol Empire was the biggest land empire on Earth;

2. Ulaanbaatar, Mongolia's capital, means "Red Hero";

3. Mongolians add salt to their milk tea;

4. Shaking hands is a form of apology in Mongolia;

5. It is considered impolite to show your wrists to someone. So the Mongolians always keep the sleeves rolled down.

Spot 16 differences

In the upper picture:

The (1)**s**_ _ _ _ _ is coming out of the chimney. The (2)**m**_ _ is turned the other way. There is a (3)**s**_ _ _ _ _ on the horse. The goat is eating a (4)**l**_ _ _. The (5)**g**_ _ _ is in the middle of the picture. The goat is in (6)**f**_ _ _ _ of the ger (house). The (7)**c**_ _ _ _ _ _ is located on the left. The right part of the ger's (8)**b**_ _ _ _ _ is not decorated.

In the bottom picture:

The ger is (9)**b**_ _ _ _ _. There is a (10)**m**_ _ _ instead of the stallion. The (11)**r**_ _ _ is black. The goat's (12)**h**_ _ _ _ is of different colour. There is a (13)**s**_ _ _ on the goat's hair. There is a (11)**b**_ _ _ on the neck of the goat. There is an (15)**e**_ _ _ _ _ in the sky. There are no (16)**m**_ _ _ _ _ _ _ _ on man's face.

The Netherlands

Capital City: Amsterdam
Official language: Dutch

Interesting facts

1. The Netherlands mean "Low Country" in Dutch. About half of its surface area is less than 1 metre above sea level;

2. The Netherlands is often called Holland. But Holland is only two out of twelve provinces;

3. There are over 1200 windmills all over the country. The oldest mill dates back to the 15th Century;

4. There are over 22 million bicycles in the country and only 17 million residents;

5. Klompen (clogs, or wooden shoes) is one of the symbols of the Netherlands. The clogs were worn by the working class and farmers to protect their feet.

Spot 16 differences

In the upper picture:

The (1)w_ _ _ _ _ _ _ is on the right. The (2)b_ _ _ is violet. There is a (3)h_ _ _ on the bike. There is a (4)l_ _ _ in the picture. The (5)s_ _ _ is turned towards the mill. There are two types of tulips behind the (6)b_ _. The boy on the bike is in the (7) m_ _ _ _ _ of the picture. The (8)b_ _ _ _ _ is in the back of the bike.

In the bottom picture:

The (9)b_ _ _ _ _ of the mill are in different position. The windmill is (10)b_ _ _ _ _.The (11)s_ _ _ is in the middle of the picture. There is a (12)g_ _ _ _ and two (13)g_ _ _ _ _ _ _ near the windmill. There are (14)t_ _ _ _ tulips near the windmill. The boy has (15) b_ _ _ _ _ _ _ pants. There are purple tulips next to the (16)b_ _.

Norway

Capital City: Oslo
Official language: Norwegian

Interesting facts

1. The previous name of Oslo is Christiania - after the Danish King Christian IV, who rebuilt the city after a great fire;

2. During Norway's Polar Nights, the sun is up for only 3 hours a day in some parts;

3. Every Christmas Oslo sends a Christmas tree to the cities of London, Edinburgh, New York and Washington;

4. Norwegians invented skiing some 4000 years ago;

5. Cheese slicer was invented by a Norwegian.

Spot 17 differences

In the upper picture:

There is a (1)**p**_ _ _ in the picture. The Viking caught a (2)**f**_ _ _.
Moomintroll has a (3)**f**_ _ _ _ coloured Norwegian flag. There
are fish in the (4)**b**_ _ _. There is a (5)**s**_ _ _ _ _ in the river. There
is stone (6)**t**_ _ _ _ on the bank of the river. The fishing lines
are (7)**b**_ _ _ _, not grey. There are (8)**m**_ _ _ _ _ _ _ _ _ under
the pine.

In the bottom picture:

There are two (9)**m**_ _ _ _ _ _ _ _ _ in the picture. The boat is (10)
g_ _ _ not blue. The Viking has (11)**r**_ _ hair. There is a (12)**m**_ _ _ _
on the bank of the river. The Viking shirt is (13)**b**_ _ _. The mountain
(14)**r**_ _ _ _ is located differently. There are cobblestones on the
(15)**b**_ _ _ of the river. There is a (16)**p**_ _ _ _ _ near Moomintroll.
There are (17)**b**_ _ _ _ _ _ in the grass.

Peru

Capital City: Lima
Official languages: Spanish, Aymara, and Quechua

Interesting facts

1. The source of the Amazon river is in Peru;

2. Potatoes have originated in Peru;

3. Three-quarters of the world's alpaca population lives in Peru;

4. Poncho is a traditional Latin American outwear. Peruvians receive one poncho upon becoming an adult and it is expected to last a lifetime;

5. Yellow underpants are a common gift given on New Year's Eve. Peruvians believe they bring good luck in the coming year.

Spot 14 differences

In the upper picture:

The lama is eating (1)**g**_ _ _ _. The woman is wearing beige (2) **h**_ _. There is a (3)**b**_ _ _ on the woman's back. The (4)**d**_ _ _ _ is dark blue. The colour of the (5)**l**_ _ _ is dark grey. The lama's legs are (6)**b**_ _ _ _. The baby is tied to the back with a turquoise (7) **s**_ _ _ _.

In the bottom picture:

The (8)**e**_ _ _ of the lama are of different colour. There is a (9) **n**_ _ _ _ _ _ _ on the lama's neck. The dress is (10)**g**_ _ _ _. The border pattern of the dress is a different (11)**c**_ _ _ _ _ _. Stripes on the (12)**p**_ _ _ _ _ are turquoise. The woman is not wearing (13)**s**_ _ _ _. There are (14)**s**_ _ _ _ to the temple.

Poland

Capital City: Warsaw
Official language: Polish

Interesting facts

1. The country's name comes from the name of an old Slavic tribe, the Polanie;

2. Poland's national symbol is the white-tailed eagle;

3. When a person turns 18 years old, he or she is considered an adult. Since then the name day becomes more important than a birthday;

4. Poland is one of the few countries where courteous hand kissing is still a common practice;

5. When Poles see a magpie bird, they believe someone will come to visit them.

Spot 16 differences

In the upper picture:

The woman is wearing multicoloured (1)**s**_ _ _ _ _. There are two strands of beads on the woman's (2)**c**_ _ _ _. The woman is wearing grey (3)**b**_ _ _ _ _ on her feet. The position of the woman's (4)**h**_ _ _ _ is different. The man is wearing a sleeveless (5)**j**_ _ _ _ _ _. The eagle is sitting on the man's (6)**s**_ _ _ _ _ _ _ _. The man has striped (7)**p**_ _ _ _ _. There are yellow (8)**b**_ _ _ _ _ _ _ on the jacket.

In the bottom picture:

The (9)**c**_ _ _ _ _ _ of the woman's blouse is different. The position of woman's (10)**f**_ _ _ is different. The woman's jacket has long (11)**s**_ _ _ _ _ _ _. The woman is wearing an (12)**a**_ _ _ _ _. There are no stripes on the man's (13)**b**_ _ _ _. The man's (14)**h**_ _ has a different design. The man's jacket has (15)**b**_ _ _ colour. The (16)**p**_ _ _ _ are blue.

Portugal

Capital City: Lisbon
Official language: Portuguese

Interesting facts

1. Lisbon is older than Rome;

2. Rio de Janeiro was once the capital of Portugal which meant it was the only European capital to be located outside Europe;

3. The rooster is a symbol of Portugal;

4. Vasco da Gama, a Portuguese explorer, was the first European to reach India by sea;

5. The Portuguese were the first Europeans to "discover" tea in East Asia. And later a Portuguese princess brought it over to English court.

Spot 15 differences

In the upper picture:

The (1)c_ _ _ _ _ of the man's shirt has a different design. The man's(2)b_ _ _ is tied on the other side. The man is holding both (3)h_ _ _ _ behind him. Planks of the (4)b_ _ _ _ _ are tilted. The woman's skirt is (5)b_ _ _ _. There are two types of (6)f_ _ _ _ _ _ on the apron. The (7)s_ _ _ _ is coloured differently. The woman's (8)v_ _ _ is coloured differently.

In the bottom picture:

The pattern of the man's (9)s_ _ _ _ is different. The belly of the (10)r_ _ _ _ _ _ _ is yellow. The man is wearing a (11)v_ _ _. The man's (12)f_ _ _ are parallel to each other. The woman's (13)a_ _ _ _ is black. There is a (14)p_ _ _ _ _ _ _ on the scarf. The woman is wearing a (15)h_ _.

Russia

Capital City: Moscow
Official language: Russian

Interesting facts

1. Russia is the largest country in the world in terms of territory;

2. Lake Baikal is the oldest lake in the world and it holds 20% of the world's supply of fresh water;

3. Russia is home to the coldest village in the World. The coldest recorded temperature in Oymyakon is -96 ° F (-72 ° C);

4. The Metro in St. Petersburg is the deepest subway system in the world. Its average depth reaches 100 meters!

5. People in Russia drink a lot of hot tea. They can drink 5-10 cups of tea every day.

Spot 16 differences

In the upper picture:

There are two (1)**b**_______ next to the bear. There are (2)**f**____ cones next to the samovar. The (3)**s**_____ of ushanka-hat is different. The samovar is (4)**g**___. There are (5)**c**__________ in the grass. The sundress is (6)**b**___. There is no yellow (7)**s**______ on the bow. There is no (8)**h**_____ jar near the bear.

In the bottom picture:

There is a (9)**f**_________ near the bear. There is a bundle of barankis on the bear's (10)**n**___. There is a (11)**b**___ on the samovar. The bear is holding a (12)**b**__________ in a different hand. There is only one (13)**c**___ near the samovar. The woman's (14)**p**_____ is on her front. The (15)**w**_____ is wearing a national hat (kokoshnik). There is a (16)**b**___ on the honey jar.

Scotland

Capital City: Edinburgh
Official language: English

Interesting facts

1. Edinburgh, the Scotland's capital, is a city built on seven hills. The other cities in this "7 hill club" are Rome, Moscow, and Madrid;

2. Scotland is the birthplace of golf – it has been played there since the 15th century;

3. Haggis is Scotland's iconic national dish. It is a type of pudding composed of the liver, heart, and lungs of a sheep (or other animal);

4. In the north eastern Scotland, they call girls – "quines" and boys – "louns";

5. Arthur's Seat - one of the hill in Edinburgh is actually an extinct volcano.

Spot 16 differences

In the upper picture:

There are two storm (1)**c**_ _ _ _ _ in the sky. The kilt is coloured purple not (2)**r**_ _. The Scott is blowing the (3)**b**_ _ _ _ _ _ _. There is a (4)**s**_ _ _ _ on the bank of the lake. The socks are (5)**g**_ _ _ _ not white. There is a (6)**f**_ _ _ in the lake. The ridge of Nessie is (7) **o**_ _ _ _ _ _. Nessie has green (8)**e**_ _ _ _ _ _ _.

In the bottom picture:

There is the Scottish (9)**f**_ _ _ on the belt. The bagpipes is coloured (10)**g**_ _ _ _. There is (11)**h**_ _ _ _ _ _ _ instead of sheep. There is heather in front of the (12)**S**_ _ _ _. There are more heather (13)**f**_ _ _ _ _ _ _ on the left from the Scott. Nessie is holding a (14)**f**_ _ _ in the hands. There are two (15)**c**_ _ _ _ _ _ in the sky. There is a (16)**w**_ _ _ _ _ _ _ _ _ in the mountains.

Spain

Capital City: Madrid
Official language: Spanish

Interesting facts

1. Spanish is the world's second-most spoken native language;

2. The national anthem of Spain has no words;

3. People who live in Madrid are often called "gatos" meaning cats because they sleep all day and are out all night;

4. The Eiffel Tower that is in Paris was originally planned to be built in Barcelona;

5. Tomatoes, potatoes, avocadoes, tobacco, and cacao, were first brought to Spain, then spread around the world.

Spot 18 differences

In the upper picture:

There are spots on the bull's (1)**s**_ _ _. The bull's (2)**f**_ _ _ _ _ _ is black. The (3)**e**_ _ _ of the bull are wide open. The pattern of the matador's (4)**s**_ _ _ is different. There is a red (5)**b**_ _ _ on the matador's waist. The muleta in the hands of the (6)**m**_ _ _ _ _ _ _ is shorter. There are (7)**s**_ _ _ _ on the muleta's stick. The different position of the woman's (8)**h**_ _ _ _. The woman's (9)**h**_ _ _ is longer.

In the bottom picture:

The bull's skin is (10)**b**_ _ _ _. The tip on the (11)**t**_ _ _ of the bull is lighter. There is no (12)**r**_ _ _ in the bull's nose. The matador's suit is (13)**p**_ _ _ _ _. There is a (14)**h**_ _ on matador's head. The matador's socks are (15)**o**_ _ _ _ _ _. The woman is wearing a white (16)**b**_ _ _ _ _ and a (17)**s**_ _ _ _. The (18)**f**_ _ _ _ _ _ in the woman's head is all red.

Sweden

Capital City: Stockholm
Official language: Swedish

Interesting facts

1. 89% of people in Sweden speak English;

2. In Sweden good drivers can take part in a lottery funded by bad driving fines;

3. In Sweden there is a prohibition on painting houses without permission from the government;

4. The official Twitter account of Sweden is given to a random citizen every week to manage;

5. There's a golf club on the border of Sweden and Finland: half the holes are in one country and half in the other.

Spot 21 differences

In the upper picture:
The woman is on the (1)**l**_ _ _ side. There are (2)**f**_ _ _ _ _ _ in the woman's hair. The woman is holding her hand (3)**b**_ _ _ _ _ her back. The woman's (4)**p**_ _ _ _ _ are shorter. The (5)**p**_ _ _ _ _ _ of the apron is different. There are (6)**l**_ _ _ _ on the apron. The man is wearing a (7)**s**_ _ _ _ on his neck. The man has (8)**b**_ _ _ _ _ hair. The man is wearing a blue (9)**v**_ _ _. The man's (10)**s**_ _ _ _ are white. There are laces on the man's (11)**p**_ _ _ _.

In the bottom picture:
The (12)**w**_ _ _ _ _ is on the right. The woman has a (13)**h**_ _ on her head. The upper part of the (14)**d**_ _ _ _ is different. The (15) **c**_ _ _ _ _ _ of woman's blouse has a laces. There is a (16)**b**_ _ on the woman's waist. The man is wearing a (17)**j**_ _ _ _ _ instead of the vest. The man's hat is (18)**y**_ _ _ _ _ _. The man's (19)**b**_ _ _ is coloured as Swedish flag. There are buckles on the (20)**s**_ _ _ _. The wooden horse is (21)**r**_ _.

Switzerland

Capital City: Bern
Official languages: German, French, Italy, Romansh

Interesting facts

1. Switzerland has a square flag;

2. Switzerland has more than 1,500 lakes. You are never more than 10 miles from a lake;

3. The children go to school from 4 years old;

4. Switzerland is very protective of people experiencing neighbourly noise. In fact, it's against the law to flush a toilet after 10 pm,

5. and no mowing the lawn, no laundry hanging outside, no hammering on Sundays.

Spot 17 differences

In the upper picture:

There are five (1)**m**_________. There is a small (2)**b**______ on the dog's neck. The (3)**h**_ _ on the woman's head looks different. The apron is (4)**p**_ _ _. The dress is (5)**b**_ _ _. There is a (6)**f**_______ in the man's hat. There is a locket on the woman's (7)**c**_____. The man is not wearing a (8)**v**_ _ _. The jacket has short (9)**s**_______.

In the bottom picture:

There is a (10)**c**_ _ in the picture. The (11)**s**____ on the right mountain is tilted in the other direction. There is a (12)**s**_ _ _ on the dog's back. There is a cape on the (13)**s**________ of a woman. The jacket has no (14)**p**______. There are (15)**f**______ behind the dog. There is a (16)**f**______ pattern on the trembite. The dog has a (17)**c**______.

Thailand

Capital City: Bangkok
Official languages: Thai

Interesting facts

1. Before 1939 Thailand was known as Siam. And then it changed its name to Thailand.

2. It's impossible to hang Thailand's national flag upside down. The flag is symmetrical, so it'll look the same even when you turn it upside down;

3. Bangkok is the world's hottest city. The median air temperature in Bangkok is 28ºC;

4. In the past, all young men in Thailand, including royalty, became Buddhist monks before they turned twenty;

5. Driving car or scooter with no shirt in Thailand is illegal, and the punishment can include prison time.

Spot 17 differences

In the upper picture:

Elephant's (1)f_ _ _ _ _ _ is thinner. The quantity and location of the wrinkles on the (2)t_ _ _ _ are different. The elephant's (3)m_ _ _ _ is different. There is a (4)s_ _ _ on the elephant leg. There are two (5)w_ _ _ _ _ _ _ on the elephant's leg. The elephant is holding a (6)p_ _ _ _ _ _ _ _ in the trunk. The (7)t_ _ _ _ has a pattern. The woman is standing on the different (8)l_ _. There is a (9)s_ _ _ _ _ of Buddha behind the woman.

In the bottom picture:

The (10)e_ _ _ of the elephant are different. There are two (11) p_ _ _ _ _ _ _ _ _ _ on the table. The palm tree is in the (12)c_ _ _ _ _ of the picture. There are more (13)l_ _ _ _ _ on a palm tree. The (14) t_ _ _ _ is closer to the elephant. The woman is wearing a (15)c_ _ _ _ _ _ _, not a dress. The woman's (16)h_ _ _ _ are raised up. The (17)b_ _ _ _ _ _ _ _ is on the other leg.

Turkey

Capital City: Ankara
Official languages: Turkish

Interesting facts

1. The capital of Turkey is Ankara and not Istanbul as many believe;

2. One part of Istanbul lies in Europe and the other part lies in Asia;

3. The Turks believe that blue eyes give off the most negative energy. The Nazar or the Evil Eye is a popular eye-shaped amulet made of glass. It protects you against the evil eye;

4. Throwing a cup of water behind you before setting off for a journey is considered a good luck In Turkey;

5. Have you ever tried chicken breast pudding with milk, sugar and dusted with cinnamon? It is popular dessert in Turkey.

Spot 15 differences

In the upper picture:

The carpet has a different (1)**s**_ _ _ _. There is a (2)**t**_ _ _ _ _ on the fez(hat). The man's (3)**m**_ _ _ _ _ _ _ _ is curled. The man holds the a tulip-shaped (4)**g**_ _ _ _. The (5)**s**_ _ _ _ _ _ on the man's shirt are rolled up. There is a pattern on the side of the (6)**t**_ _ _ _. There is a picture of (7)**f**_ _ _ _ _ _ on the surface of the table.

In the bottom picture:

The carpet has different (8)**c**_ _ _ _ _ and (9)**p**_ _ _ _ _ _ _. The (10) **f**_ _ on the man's head is bigger. The (11)**s**_ _ _ _ _ _ _ _ are orange. The (12)**t**_ _ _ _ _ is grey. There are (13)**l**_ _ _ _ on the shirt. There are (14)**s**_ _ _ _ _ on the table. The table's (15)**l**_ _ is of a different shape.

USA

Capital City: Washington
Official language: English

Interesting facts

1. New York City started as a Dutch colony called New Amsterdam;

2. The USA is the only country in the world that has all of the Earth's five climate zones: tropical, dry, temperate, continental and polar;

3. Alaska is the only state in the US which you can type with letters all in one keyboard row;

4. Disneyland does not sell chewing gum as Walt Disney did not want guests inconvenienced by stepping on gum purchased in the park;

5. Fines for cactus graffiti in Arizona run up to $5,000.

Spot 18 differences

In the upper picture:

The horse is (1)**g**_ _ _. The horse's mane and (2)**t**_ _ _ are brown. The bull's (3)**h**_ _ _ _ are yellow. There is no pattern on the (4)**s**_ _ _ _. The man's hat is (5)**g**_ _ _ _.The man is holding a (6)**l**_ _ _ _ in his right hand. The man is wearing a plaid (7)**s**_ _ _ _. There is no (8)**s**_ _ _ _ _ on the horse. The horse reins are (9) **b**_ _ _ _.

In the bottom picture:

There is a (10)**s**_ _ _ on the horse's head. There is a (11)**c**_ _ instead of the bull. The cow's (12)**t**_ _ _ is raised up. The (13)**g**_ _ _ _ is growing near the cow. The man's (14)**s**_ _ _ _ is coloured as US flag. The man is wearing a (15)**v**_ _ _ instead of a jacket. There is no fringe on the man's (16)**b**_ _ _ _. The rider has his (17)**f**_ _ _ in the stirrups. The cow is chewing (18)**g**_ _ _ _.

Clues

In the upper picture:
There are two (1)**bushes** behind the surfer. There is a (2)**baby** in the kangaroo's pocket. There is (3)**hair** under the bandana. There is a (4)**wave** in the sea. There is a white (5)**spot** on the kangaroo's tail. The surfer's (6) **nose** is bigger. There is a white spot on the kangaroo's (7)**head**.

In the bottom picture:
The (8)**sun** is on the right. There is an (9)**eucalyptus** tree. The colour of the (10)**bandana** on the surfer's head. The colour of the (11)**board** the surfer holds. The length of the kanagaroo's (12)**tail**. The (13)**colour** and the (14)**length** of swimming trunks. The colour of the (15) **eyes** is different.

In the upper picture:
The feathers of the dress are of different (1)**colours**. The woman is wearing (2)**earrings**. The top on the woman is (3)**pink**. The woman is wearing different (4)**shoes**. The (5)**baloons** are of different colours. The design and the (6)**colour** of the man's hat is different. The man is wearing a (7)**shirt** of different design and colour. There is a (8) **belt** on the man's waist. There is a maraca in the (9)**hand** of the man.

In the bottom picture:
The woman has a different (10)**hat**. The top on the woman has a different (11) **design** The woman is wearing a burgundy (12)**skirt**. The quantity of (13)**baloons**. The man is holding the (14)**baloons** in the other hand. The man is wearing a light (15)**blue** jumpsuit. The man is wearing (16)**shoes**. There are two (17)**dogs** in the picture.

Clues

Page 7

In the upper picture:

There is a different (1)**shape** of the gate. There is a (2)**green** pompom on the beaver's hat. The beaver has shields of different (3)**colour**. The (4)**puck** is near the player, not in the net. The colour of the beaver's (5)**stick** is different. There is a blue (6)**stripe** on the player sweater. The maple (7)**leaf** is yellow. The beaver has two (8)**teeth** not one.

In the bottom picture:

The corners of the gate cross-bars are (9)**red**. The colour of beaver's (10)**tail** is different. There is a brown spot on the beaver's (11)**paw**. The stick's lacing has different (12)**colour**. There is a (13)**medal** on the player's chest. The (14)**helmet** on the player's head is grey. The beaver has brown (15)**skates**.

Page 9

In the upper picture:

The woman's (1)**dress** is red. The man's plait is located on the other (2)**shoulder**. There are two (3)**dragons** on the umbrella. The woman is holding the (4)**umbrella** in the other hand. The man's hat is (5)**green**. The man has a sparse (6)**beard**. The man's (7)**pants** are red. There are blue and green stripes on the edge of the (8)**umbrella**.

In the bottom picture:

The (9)**robe** of the man is red. The man's plait is (10)**thinner** and shorter. The pagoda has one less (11)**tier**. The (12)**pattern** of the dress is different. There are two separate (13)**windows** on the ground floor of the pagoda. The man has white cuffs on his (14)**sleeves**. The button facing on the robe is (15)**blue**. There is no (16)**tea** tree near the man.

Clues

In the upper picture:
The woman's (1)**jacket** is black. The (2)**apron** has two laces. The woman is holding (3)**flowers**. Woman's shoes are (4)**red** not blue. The boy has green (5)**socks**. The boy is holding a (6)**blue** Lego brick. The boy is holding a (7)**cookie** in the other hand. The woman's (8)**hair** is tied up in a bun.

In the bottom picture:
The woman is wearing a (9)**scarf**. The jacket of the woman has short (10)**sleeves**. There is a (11)**basket** in the woman's hand. The woman's (12)**hand** is raised. The boy is wearing long (13)**pants**. The boy's right hand is on his (14)**waist**. The woman is wearing a (15)**hat**. There are two rows of (16)**buttons** on the boy's vest.

In the upper picture:
The guard post is (1)**blue** not green. There are two (2)**stripes** on the post rim. The man is holding a (3)**bulldog** not dachshund. The man is holding a brown (4)**umbrella**, not a red one. There are (5)**checks** on the jacket. There is a (6)**pocket** on the jacket. There is the (7)**sun** and one (8)**cloud** in the sky.

In the bottom picture:
The roof of the post is (9)**yellow**. There are yellow (10)**stripes** on the post roof. The guard is (11)**inside** the post. There are storm (12)**clouds**. The (13)**umbrella** is opened. The jacket is (14)**blue** not green. The pants are green not (15)**brown**. The (16)**pants** are not creased.

Clues

In the upper picture:
The deer's antlers are (1)**grey**. There is a pattern on the (2)**hat**. There is no (3)**snow** on the top of the fir tree. The (4)**smoke** is coming out of the chimney. There are two (5)**windows** on the facade of the building on the second floor. There is a (6)**bucket** on the snowman. The (7)**snowman** looks towards the barrel. There are two (8)**buttons** on the snowman.

On the bottom picture:
The antlers have a different (9)**shape**. The (10)**barrel** is smaller. There is a fir tree on the (11)**hill**. There are two (12)**fir trees** near the house. There is a (13)**sleigh** in front of the house. There is a (14)**hat** on the snowman. The snowman has (15)**twigs** as hands. The deer has a grey (16)**nose**.

In the upper picture:
Eiffel Tower is in the (1)**middle** of the picture. The woman is wearing a red top and an (2)**orange** skirt . The woman is wearing blue (3)**scarf**. The woman has different (4)**hairdo**. There is no baguette in the (5)**basket**. The bike is (6)**purple**. There is a (7)**watch** on the woman's wrist. There is French (8)**flag** on the Eiffel Tower.

In the bottom picture:
The man and the woman swapped (9)**places**. The woman is wearing a pink (10)**dress**. The man is wearing an (11)**orange** beret. The man is eating a (12)**croissant**. The man's pant (13)**leg** is rolled up. Man's (14)**scarf** is tied differently. There is a (15)**bottle** in the basket. The bike's handles are (16)**green**.

Clues

In the upper picture:

There are two (1)**houses** in the picture. There are no (2)**flowers** under the attic window. The (3)**door** is red not green. The woman is wearing a (4)**hat**. The pants are (5)**brown**. The (6)**pants** are short. There are no folds on the (7)**apron**.

In the bottom picture:

There are two separate (8)**windows** on the ground floor. There is a (9)**table** in front of the house. There is a (10)**tree** behind the Germans. The (11)**feather** is on the other side of the hat. There are two (12)**buttons** on the pants. The woman is holding a (13)**glass** of beer. There are two bundles of (14)**sausages**.

Page 21

In the upper picture:

The snake charmer folded his (1)**legs** differently. The (2)**shirt** has blue buttons. There are buttons on the (3)**sleeve**. The old man has along (4)**beard**. The (5)**elephant** is looking in the different direction. There is a (6)**pad** under the snake charmer. There is no (7)**T-shirt** under the charmer's shirt. There are six wrinkles on the elephant (8)**trunk**. The charmer's hat is (9)**blue**.

In the bottom picture:

The shirt of the snake charmer is (10)**orange**. There are only two (11)**buttons** on the shirt. The (12)**T-shirt** of the old man is light blue. The elephant's (13)**tail** is located differently. The elephant's (14)**fringe** is thicker. The snake is (15)**closer** to the charmer. The shirt is covering man's (16)**legs**. The charmer has a (17)**mustache**.

Clues

Page 23

In the upper picture:
The (1)**Tower** of Pisa is on the right. The (2)**car** is red not yellow. There is a (3)**pizza** in the man's hand. The pants are (4)**green** not blue. The scarf coloured as Italian (5)**flag**. The (6)**man** has a fringe. The colour of the (7)**shoes** is different. There is a (8)**logo** on the car door.

In the bottom picture:
The (9)**car** is on the right. The (10)**headlights** of the car are smaller. The man's (11)**pants** are shorter. The man's (12)**shirt** is red not blue. Light blue dots on the rim of the (13)**plate**. The man's (14)**hair** is shorter. The shape of (15)**eyebrows** is different.

Page 25

In the upper picture:
The (1)**kimono** of the woman is pink. The (2)**pattern** of the fan is different. The woman has different (3)**hairdo**. The belt is (4)**pink**. The shape of the (5)**tree** is different. The (6)**stone** garden is on the right side of the picture. The man is in the (7)**middle** of the picture. The woman's (8)**shoes** are pink.

In the bottom picture:
The pattern of the (9)**kimono** is different. There is a (10)**hairpin** in the woman's hair. The (11)**belt** of the kimono is different. There are two (12)**trees** behind the woman. There are more (13)**stones** in the stone garden. The (14)**smoke** is coming from Fudji. There are stripes on the man's (15)**pants**. The scabbard is (16)**black**.

Clues

In the upper picture:
The sombrero is (1)**beige**. The (2)**design** of the sombrero is different. The (3)**shirt** is multicoloured. The man is wearing a (4)**yellow** band. The (5)**head** of the man is turned into a different direction. There are less appendages on the left (6)**cactus**. There are two (7)**flowers** on the right cactus. The sun is on the (8)**right** part of the picture.

In the bottom picture:
The (9)**sombrero** has a different pattern. The man is wearing a (10)**jacket**. The pants are (11)**grey**. The lampas have a different (12)**colour**. The man is holding a (13)**taco** instead of maraca. There are no small (14)**cactus** with a (15)**flower** on the left. The man has long and thin (16)**mustache**.

In the upper picture:
The (1)**smoke** is coming out of the chimney. The (2)**man** is turned the other way. There is a (3)**saddle** on the horse. The goat is eating a (4)**leaf**. The (5)**goat** is in the middle of the picture. The goat is in (6)**front** of the ger (house). The (7)**chimney** is located on the left. The right part of the ger's (8)**bottom** is not decorated.

In the bottom picture:
The ger is (9)**beige**. There is a (10)**mare** instead of the stallion. The (11)**robe** is black. The goat's (12)**hair** is of different colour. There is a (13)**spot** on the goat's hair. There is a (14)**bell** on the neck of the goat. There is an (15)**eagle** in the sky. There are no (16)**mustache** on man's face.

Clues

In the upper picture:
The (1)**windmill** is on the right. The (2)**bike** is violet. There is a (3)**horn** on the bike. There is a (4)**lake** in the picture. The (5)**swan** is turned towards the mill. There are two types of tulips behind the (6)**boy**. The boy on the bike is in the (7)**middle** of the picture. The (8)**basket** is in the back of the bike.

In the bottom picture:
The (9)**blades** of the mill are in different position. The windmill is (10)**beige**.The (11)**swan** is in the middle of the picture. There is a (12)**goose** and two (13)**goslings** near the windmill. There are (14)**three** tulips near the windmill. The boy has (15)**burgundy** pants. There are purple tulips next to the (16)**boy**.

In the upper picture:
There is a (1)**pine** in the picture. The Viking caught a (2)**fish**. Moomintroll has a (3)**float** coloured Norwegian flag. There are fish in the (4)**boat**. There is a (5)**stone** in the river. There is stone (6)**tower** on the bank of the river. The fishing lines are (7)**brown**, not grey. There are (8)**mushrooms** under the pine.

In the bottom picture:
There are two (9)**mountains** in the picture. The boat is (10)**grey** not blue. The Viking has (11)**red** hair. There is a (12)**moose** on the bank of the river. The Viking shirt is (13)**blue**. The mountain (14)**river** is located differently. There are cobblestones on the (15)**bank** of the river. There is a (16)**paddle** near Moomintroll. There are (17)**berries** in the grass.

Clues

In the upper picture:
The lama is eating (1)**grass**. The woman is wearing beige (2)**hat**. There is a (3)**baby** on the woman's back. The (4)**dress** is dark blue. The colour of the (5)**lama** is dark grey. The lama's legs are (6)**brown**. The baby is tied to the back with a turquoise (7)**scarf**.

In the bottom picture:
The (8)**ears** of the lama are of different colour. There is a (9)**neckless** on the lama's neck. The dress is (10)**green**. The border pattern of the dress is a different (11)**colour**. Stripes on the (12)**poncho** are turquoise. The woman is not wearing (13)**socks**. There are (14)**steps** to the temple.

In the upper picture:
The woman is wearing multicoloured (1)**skirt**. There are two strands of beads on the woman's (2)**chest**. The woman is wearing grey (3)**boots** on her feet. The position of the woman's (4)**hands** is different. The man is wearing a sleeveless (5)**jacket**. The eagle is sitting on the man's (6)**shoulder**. The man has striped (7)**pants**. There are yellow (8)**buttons** on the jacket.

In the bottom picture:
The (9)**collar** of the woman's blouse is different. The position of woman's (10)**feet** is different. The woman's jacket has long (11)**sleeves** . The woman is wearing an (12)**apron**. There are no stripes on the man's (13)**belt**. The man's (14)**hat** has a different design. The man's jacket has (15)**blue** colour. The (16)**pants** are blue.

Clues

Page 39

In the upper picture:
The (1)**collar** of the man's shirt has a different design. The man's(2)**belt** is tied on the other side. The man is holding both (3)**hands** behind him. Planks of the (4)**barrel** are tilted. The woman's skirt is (5)**black**. There are two types of (6)**flowers** on the apron. The (7)**scarf** is coloured differently. The woman's (8)**vest** is coloured differently.

In the bottom picture:
The pattern of the man's (9)**shirt** is different. The belly of the (10)**rooster** is yellow. The man is wearing a (11)**vest**. The man's (12)**feet** are parallel to each other. The woman's (13)**apron** is black. There is a (14)**pattern** on the scarf. The woman is wearing a (15)**hat**.

Page 41

In the upper picture:
There are two (1)**birches** next to the bear. There are (2)**four** cones next to the samovar. The (3)**shape** of ushanka-hat is different. The samovar is (4)**grey**. There are (5)**camomiles** in the grass. The sundress is (6)**blue**. There is no yellow (7)**stripe** on the bow . There is no (8)**honey** jar near the bear.

In the bottom picture:
There is a (9)**fir tree** near the bear. There is a bundle of barankis on the bear's (10)**neck**. There is a (11)**boot** on the samovar. The bear is holding a (12)**balalaika** in a different hand. There is only one (13)**cup** near the samovar. The woman's (14)**plait** is on her front. The (15)**woman** is wearing a national hat (kokoshnik). There is a (16)**bee** on the honey jar.

Clues

Page 43

In the upper picture:
There are two storm (1)**clouds** in the sky. The kilt is coloured purple not (2)**red**. The Scott is blowing the (3)**bagpipes**. There is a (4)**sheep** on the bank of the lake. The socks are (5)**green** not white. There is a (6)**fish** in the lake. The ridge of Nessie is (7)**orange**. Nessie has green (8)**eyelids**.

In the bottom picture:
There is the Scottish (9)**flag** on the belt. The bagpipes is coloured (10)**green**. There is (11)**heather** instead of sheep. There is heather in front of the (12)**Scott**. There are more heather (13)**flowers** on the left from the Scott. Nessie is holding a (14)**fish** in the hands. There are two (15)**clouds** in the sky. There is a (16)**waterfall** in the mountains.

Page 45

In the upper picture:
There are spots on the bull's (1)**skin**. The bull's (2)**fringe** is black. The (3)**eyes** of the bull are wide open. The pattern of the matador's (4)**suit** is different. There is a red (5)**belt** on the matador's waist. The muleta in the hands of the (6)**matador** is shorter. There are (7)**spots** on the muleta's stick. The different position of the woman's (8)**hands**. The woman's (9)**hair** is longer.

In the bottom picture:
The bull's skin is (10)**brown**. The tip on the (11)**tail** of the bull is lighter. There is no (12)**ring** in the bull's nose. The matador's suit is (13)**purple**. There is a (14)**hat** on matador's head. The matador's socks are (15)**orange**. The woman is wearing a white (16)**blouse** and a (17)**skirt**. The (18)**flower** in the woman's head is all red.

Clues

In the upper picture:
The woman is on the (1)**left** side. There are (2)**flowers** in the woman's hair. The woman is holding her hand (3)**behind** her back. The woman's (4)**plaits** are shorter. The (5)**pattern** of the apron is different. There are (6)**laces** on the apron. The man is wearing a (7)**scarf** on his neck. The man has (8)**blond** hair. The man is wearing a blue (9)**vest**. The man's (10)**socks** are white. There are laces on the man's (11)**pants**.

In the bottom picture:
The (12)**woman** is on the right. The woman has a (13)**hat** on her head. The upper part of the (14)**dress** is different. The (15)**collar** of woman's blouse has a laces. There is a (16)**bag** on the woman's waist. The man is wearing a (17)**jacket** instead of the vest. The man's hat is (18)**yellow**. The man's (19)**belt** is coloured as Swedish flag. There are buckles on the (20)**shoes**. The wooden horse is (21)**red**.

Page 49

In the upper picture:
There are five (1)**mountains**. There is a small (2)**barrel** on the dog's neck. The (3)**hat** on the woman's head looks different. The apron is (4)**pink**. The dress is (5)**blue**. There is a (6)**feather** in the man's hat. There is a locket on the woman's (7)**chest**. The man is not wearing a (8)**vest**. The jacket has short (9)**sleeves**.

In the bottom picture:
There is a (10)**cow** in the picture. The (11)**snow** on the right mountain is tilted in the other direction. There is a (12)**spot** on the dog's back. There is a cape on the (13)**shoulders** of a woman. The jacket has no (14)**pockets**. There are (15)**flowers** behind the dog. There is a (16)**flower** pattern on the trembite. The dog has a (17)**collar**.

Clues

In the upper picture:
Elephant's (1)**fringe** is thinner. The quantity and location of the wrinkles on the (2)**trunk** are different. The elephant's (3)**mouth** is different. There is a (4)**spot** on the elephant leg. There are two (5)**wrinkles** on the elephant's leg. The elephant is holding a (6)**pineapple** in the trunk. The (7)**table** has a pattern. The woman is standing on the different (8)**leg**. There is a (9)**statue** of Buddha behind the woman.

In the bottom picture:
The (10)**eyes** of the elephant are different. There are two (11)**pineapples** on the table. The palm tree is in the (12)**center** of the picture. There are more (13)**leaves** on a palm tree. The (14) **table** is closer to the elephant. The woman is wearing a (15)**costume**, not a dress. The woman's (16)**hands** are raised up. The (17)**bracelet** is on the other leg.

In the upper picture:
The carpet has a different (1)**shape**. There is a (2)**tassel** on the fez (hat). The man's (3)**mustache** is curled. The man is holding a tulip-shaped (4)**glass**. The (5)**sleaves** on the man's shirt are rolled up. There is a pattern on the side of the (6)**table**. There is a picture of (7)**flowers** on the surface of the table.

In the bottom picture:
The carpet has different (8)**colour** and (9)**pattern**. The (10)**fez** on the man's head is bigger. The (11)**slippers** are orange. The (12)**teapot** is grey. There are (13)**laces** on the shirt. There are (14)**sweets** on the table. The table's (15)**leg** is of a different shape.

Clues

In the upper picture:

The horse is (1)**grey**. The horse's mane and (2)**tail** are brown. The bull's (3)**horns** are yellow. There is no pattern on the (4)**scarf**. The man's hat is (5)**green**. The man is holding a (6)**lasso** in his right hand. The man is wearing a plaid (7)**shirt**. There is no (8)**saddle** on the horse. The horse reins are (9)**brown**.

In the bottom picture:

There is a (10)**spot** on the horse's head. There is a (11)**cow** instead of the bull. The cow's (12)**tail** is raised up. The (13)**grass** is growing near the cow. The man's (14)**scarf** is coloured as US flag. The man is wearing a (15)**vest** instead of a jacket. There is no fringe on the man's (16)**boots**. The rider has his (17)**feet** in the stirrups. The cow is chewing (18)**grass**.

Notes

Notes

ISBN 978-5-6047535-0-7

www.funnylanguages.com